FLUTE FOR KIDS

FLUTE FOR KIDS
Christmas Carols, Classical Music, Nursery Rhymes, Traditional & Folk Songs!

FLUTE FOR KIDS:
Christmas Carols, Classical Music, Nursery Rhymes, Traditional & Folk Songs!

© JAVIER MARCÓ

ISBN-13:978-1499243468
ISBN-10:1499243464

Contents

Playing Guide	7
Aloutte	13
Amazing Grace	14
America The Beautiful	15
Arroz Con Leche	16
Aserrín, Aserrán	17
Aura Lee	18
Cielito Lindo	19
For He's a Jolly Good Fellow	20
Frere Jacques	21
Go Tell Aunt Rhody	22
Good Morning To All	23
Greensleeves	24
Jingle Bells	25
La Cucaracha	26
La Donna è Mobile	27
Las Mañanitas	28
London Bridge Is Falling Down	29
Mary Had A Little Lamb	30
Menuett in G	31
My Bonnie Lies Over The Ocean	32
Ode an die Freude	33
Oh! Susanna	34
Old MacDonald Had a Farm	35
Row Row Row Your Boat	36
Scarborough Fair	37
Stille Nacht, heilige Nacht	38
Sur le Pont d'Avignon	39
The House Of The Rising Sun	40
The Star-Spangled Banner	41
Twinkle Twinkle Little Star	42
Un Elefante Se Balanceaba	43
We Wish You A Merry Christmas	44
When Johnny Comes Marching Home	45
When the Saints Go Marching In	46
Wiegenlied	47
Yankee Doodle	48

Playing guide

Standard notation
Notes are written on a Staff.

Staff
The staff consists of five lines and four spaces, on which notes symbols are placed.

Clef
A clef assigns an individual note to a certain line. The **Treble Clef** or **G Clef** is used for the flute.

This clef indicates the position of the note G which is on the second line from the bottom.

Note
A note is a sign used to represent the relative pitch of a sound. There are seven notes:
A, B, C, D, E, F and G.

Ledger lines
The ledger lines are used to inscribe notes outside the lines and spaces of the staff.

Accidentals
An accidental is a symbol to raise or lower the pitch of a note.

♯ sharp   Next note up half step.
♭ flat   Next note down half step.
♮ natural   Cancels a flat or a sharp.

Note values
A **note value** is used to indicate the duration of a note. A **rest** is an interval of silence, marked by a sign indicating the length of the pause. Each rest corresponds to a particular note value.

Dotted note
A dotted note is a note with a small dot written after it. The dot adds half as much again to the basic note's duration.

Tie
A tie is a curved line connecting the heads of two notes of the same pitch, indicating that they are to be played as a single note with a duration equal to the sum of the individual notes' note values.

Bars or Measures
The staff is divided into equal segments of time consisting of the same number of beats, called bar or measures.

Time signature
Time signature consists of two numbers, the upper number specifies how many beats (or counts) are in each measure, and the lower number tells us the note value which represents one beat.

Example: 4/4 means four quarters, or four beats per measure with a quarter note receiving one beat or count.

Key signature
A Key signature is a group of accidentals, generally written at the beginning of a score immediately after the clef, and shows which notes always get sharps or flats. Accidentals on the lines and spaces in the key signature affect those notes throughout the piece unless there is a natural sign.

First and second endings
The section should be repeated from the beginning, and number brackets above the bars indicate which to played the first time (1), which to play the second time (2).

Dynamics
Dynamics refers to the volume of the notes.

p   (piano), meaning soft.
mp (mezzo-piano), meaning "moderately soft".
mf (mezzo-forte), meaning "moderately loud".
f   (forte), meaning loud.

Crescendo. A gradual increase in volume.

Decrescendo. A gradual decrease in volume.

Tempo Markings
Tempo is written at the beginning of a piece of music and indicates how slow or fast this piece should be played.

Adagio — slow and stately (66–76 bpm)

Andate — at a walking pace (76–108 bpm)

Moderato — moderately (101-110 bpm)

Allegro — fast, quickly and bright (120–139 bpm)

Allegretto — moderately fast (but less so than allegro)

Presto — extremely fast (180–200 bpm)

Articulation

Legato. Notes are played smoothly and connected.

Stacatto. Notes are played separated or detached from its neighbours by a silence.

Fermata (pause)
The note is to be prolonged at the pleasure of the performer.

Aloutte

Traditionnel

Allegro

Amazing Grace

Traditional

America The Beautiful

Samuel A. Ward

Arroz Con Leche

Tradicional

Aserrín, Aserrán

Tradicional

Aura Lee

George R. Poulton

Allegro

Cielito Lindo

Quirino Mendoza y Cortés

For He's a Jolly Good Fellow

Traditional

Allegro

Frere Jacques

Traditionnel

Allegro

Go Tell Aunt Rhody

Traditional

Allegro

Good Morning To All

Patty & Mildred J. Hill

Greensleeves

Traditional

Andante

Jingle Bells

James Lord Pierpont

La Cucaracha

Tradicional

Allegro

La Donna è Mobile

Giuseppe Verdi

Las Mañanitas

Tradicional

Allegro

London Bridge Is Falling Down

Traditional

Allegro

29

Mary Had A Little Lamb

Traditional

Presto

mf

Menuett in G

Johann Sebastian Bach

Allegretto

My Bonnie Lies Over The Ocean

Ode an die Freude

Ludwig Van Beethoven

Moderato

Oh! Susanna

Stephen Foster

Presto

Old MacDonald Had A Farm

Traditional

Row Row Row Your Boat

Traditional

Presto

Scarborough Fair

Traditional

Allegro

37

Stille Nacht, heilige Nacht

Franz Xaver Gruber

Sur le Pont d'Avignon

Traditionnel

Allegro

The House Of The Rising Sun

Traditional

Moderato

The Star-Spangled Banner

Music by John Stafford Smith

Moderato

Twinkle Twinkle Little Star

W. A. Mozart

Un Elefante Se Balanceaba

Tradicional

We Wish You A Merry Christmas

Traditional

Presto

When Johnny Comes Marching Home

Traditional

When The Saints Go Marching In

Traditional

Presto

Wiegenlied

Johannes Brahms

Adagio

Yankee Doodle

Traditional

Allegro

info@marcomusica.com

CPSIA information can be obtained
at www.ICGtesting.com
Printed in the USA
LVOW03s1023151215
466706LV00021B/897/P

9 781499 243468